CAMBRIDGE LIBRARY COLLECTION

Books of enduring scholarly value

Polar Exploration

This series includes accounts, by eye-witnesses and contemporaries, of early expeditions to the Arctic and the Antarctic. Huge resources were invested in such endeavours, particularly the search for the North-West Passage, which, if successful, promised enormous strategic and commercial rewards. Cartographers and scientists travelled with many of the expeditions, and their work made important contributions to earth sciences, climatology, botany and zoology. They also brought back anthropological information about the indigenous peoples of the Arctic region and the southern fringes of the American continent. The series further includes dramatic and poignant accounts of the harsh realities of working in extreme conditions and utter isolation in bygone centuries.

The Land of the White Bear

In June 1875, Frederick George Innes-Lillingston (1849–1904) set out for the Arctic aboard *Pandora*, a steam yacht captained by the seasoned polar explorer Allen Young (1827–1915). In this, the first of two voyages north, Young sought to make the north-west passage. His lieutenant Innes-Lillingston published this short account in 1876. It follows the voyage through to Peel Strait, where Young was forced to turn back in the face of heavy ice. On the journey home, the *Pandora* picked up the dispatches of the expedition under George Nares that was attempting to reach the North Pole. Conveying both the thrill and difficulty of the endeavour, this narrative provides a highly readable account of seafaring in extreme conditions. Also reissued in this series are two related works by Young: *Cruise of the Pandora* (1876) and *The Two Voyages of the Pandora* (1879).

T0381777

Cambridge University Press has long been a pioneer in the reissuing of out-of-print titles from its own backlist, producing digital reprints of books that are still sought after by scholars and students but could not be reprinted economically using traditional technology. The Cambridge Library Collection extends this activity to a wider range of books which are still of importance to researchers and professionals, either for the source material they contain, or as landmarks in the history of their academic discipline.

Drawing from the world-renowned collections in the Cambridge University Library and other partner libraries, and guided by the advice of experts in each subject area, Cambridge University Press is using state-of-the-art scanning machines in its own Printing House to capture the content of each book selected for inclusion. The files are processed to give a consistently clear, crisp image, and the books finished to the high quality standard for which the Press is recognised around the world. The latest print-on-demand technology ensures that the books will remain available indefinitely, and that orders for single or multiple copies can quickly be supplied.

The Cambridge Library Collection brings back to life books of enduring scholarly value (including out-of-copyright works originally issued by other publishers) across a wide range of disciplines in the humanities and social sciences and in science and technology.

The Land of
the White Bear

*Being a Short Account of the Pandora's Voyage
During the Summer of 1875*

FREDERICK GEORGE INNES-LILLINGSTON

CAMBRIDGE
UNIVERSITY PRESS

CAMBRIDGE
UNIVERSITY PRESS

University Printing House, Cambridge, CB2 8BS, United Kingdom

Published in the United States of America by Cambridge University Press, New York

Cambridge University Press is part of the University of Cambridge.
It furthers the University's mission by disseminating knowledge in the pursuit of
education, learning and research at the highest international levels of excellence.

www.cambridge.org
Information on this title: www.cambridge.org/9781108072045

© in this compilation Cambridge University Press 2014

This edition first published 1876
This digitally printed version 2014

ISBN 978-1-108-07204-5 Paperback

Finding the Dispatches.

The Cairn on the Carey Islands

THE

LAND OF THE WHITE BEAR:

BEING

A SHORT ACCOUNT OF THE 'PANDORA'S' VOYAGE
DURING THE SUMMER OF 1875.

BY

LIEUT. F. G. INNES-LILLINGSTON, R.N.
F.R.G.S.

PORTSMOUTH:
J. GRIFFIN AND CO., 2 THE HARD.

LONDON:
SIMPKIN, MARSHALL AND CO.

1876.

PREFACE.

KIND READER,—Having been asked to write a short account of our cruise to the icy regions of the North, I have endeavoured to do so. I have never attempted to write a book before, and feel that this little volume will not bear being critically read; I therefore beg of you to overlook all errors, of which, I am sure, there are many, and simply look upon it as a record of our doings during the four months we were away from home, taken from a rough journal which I kept at the time.

Whilst I am writing this, my thoughts are with our brave countrymen who are now facing all the perils, and enduring all the hardships, of an Arctic winter; and it will be very gratifying to me if this small volume should in any way help to keep awake a warm interest in their endeavours to reach the long sought for North Pole.

F. G. INNES-LILLINGSTON.

December 1875.

CONTENTS.

CHAPTER II.

THE FAR NORTH.

CHAPTER III.

" WESTWARD HO ! "

CHAPTER IV.

HOMEWARD BOUND.

THE

LAND OF THE WHITE BEAR.

———∘o⟨⟩oo———

CHAPTER I.

OUTWARD BOUND.

"The ship was cheer'd, the harbour clear'd,
　　Merrily did we drop
　　Below the kirk, below the hill,
　　Below the lighthouse top."—*Coleridge.*

ONE day last March I opened one of the
most gratifying letters it has ever been
my good fortune to receive. It was from
Captain Allen Young, asking me to join
him in a cruise to the Arctic, to try and
find some more records of the Franklin
Expedition, should he be able to get to
King William Land.

B

Though a private letter to me, I am
sure he will not mind my inserting a few
extracts from it.

It ran as follows :—

" DEAR SIR,

    " You will perhaps have heard
" that I am thinking of a cruise to the
" Arctic this season, and when I was at
" Cowes yesterday, I met my old shipmate
" Toms, who is now in your service. In
" the course of conversation he told me
" that you had sometimes thought of
" making a trip northward; so I send you
" a line to ask you if you would join me
" and bring Toms with you."

He then goes on to state the object for
which the voyage is intended.

    " I propose," he says, " to start about
" the 20th of June, to proceed up and visit

" the points of interest in West Greenland,
" and, if we can communicate with the
" government expedition, to bring home
" their despatches; then proceed to Peel
" Straits, and, if stopped there, to try
" Bellot Straits, and, finding open naviga-
" tion down Peel Straits, or Bellot Straits,
" and Franklin Channel, I propose to go on
" until stopped by ice, and in that case im-
" mediately turn back and come home.

" I do not think anything is to be
" gained by wintering, but it will be
" necessary to have a winter's provisions
" on board, besides every other preparation
" in case of accident. The grand object
" would be to sail through to Behring
" Straits in one summer, and there would
" be no advantage in doing the same thing
" in two summers.

" We know from Collinson that the

" navigation from King William Island
" on the south is always open in summer
" to Behring Straits ; also, we know, from
" this side to Bellot Straits ; the doubtful
" place is then between Bellot Straits and
" King William Island, about one hundred
" and twenty miles. If therefore stopped
" at Bellot Straits, nothing more can be
" done, but, once through Franklin Straits,
" the N.W. Passage is easy, as the natives
" told us that the channel east of King
" William Island is always open in sum-
" mer.

" This is only my idea of a trip, but if
" you would come with me, we could make
" a very pleasant cruise, and be guided
" entirely by circumstances, without com-
" mitting ourselves to any route before
" starting, but with the one idea of return-
" ing the same year, i.e. in October next.

" I have bought *Pandora*, and am going
" on with necessary repairs and outfit,
" but I have not yet decided whether I
" shall complete her or not this season,
" as this will partly depend upon my
" finding someone who will join me, and
" who would take an interest in it.

" Perhaps you would kindly let me have
" your views.

" Yours truly,

(Signed)   " ALLEN YOUNG."

I lost no time in having an interview
with Mr. Young, and my share of the
expenses having been decided on, I found
myself enrolled as one of the *Pandora*
expedition.

The pretty little *Pandora* was down
at Southampton, on the patent slip at
Day and Summer's Dockyard, being

strengthened, both internally and externally, to withstand the rude shocks she would meet with from her future enemy, the ice. Besides this strengthening, she was also having her engines and boilers thoroughly overhauled and repaired, and her topmasts and lower yards shortened, as she would not be manned by such a large crew as she used to have when a man-of-war.

Before long she was out of the shipwrights' hands, and having gone through her trial trip, which turned out very satisfactory, she was taken into the basin in the Southampton docks, and the work of " provisioning " commenced.

Waggon load after waggon load of " grub " kept on arriving, till at last old Toms scratched his head and said, " I'm blessed if I know how we're going to stow it all, sir, but we must have a try."

Well, it all got stowed somehow, and though it looked an impossibility whilst it was in railway waggons, it did not appear so very much when carefully stowed in a ship's hold.

Before the provisions arrived, we had stowed away our sledges (which we were taking in case of having to winter) between the beams on the lower deck; and besides these we had ice anchors, ice claws, saws and triangles to work them on, long poles like overgrown boathooks, and in fact everything necessary for Arctic work.

On the 24th of June 1875, the *Pandora* glided out of Southampton docks, the dock-heads being crowded with people, many of them being friends and relations of those on board.

The next day we filled up with coals,

and at 6 P.M. weighed and proceeded under steam to Portsmouth, Captain Young having promised to pay a visit to his old Commander, Admiral Sir Leopold M'Clintock, as soon as his ship was ready to start. We found that Sir Leopold had kindly kept a place for us alongside the jetty, and had sent a man out in a boat to show us where to go to ; so we were soon lashed alongside and safe for the night.

Next morning we had a great many visitors, amongst whom were Sir Leopold and Lady M'Clintock, and Admiral Richards, who take deep interest in anything connected with the Arctic.

We wanted another hand or two ; so as I had had a letter from a man, whose time was just up, on board the *Hector*, volunteering to go with us, I went on board, and through the kindness of Captain Hoskins he was enabled to get his discharge immediately, and, with *half an hour's* notice, this man, George Thorne, was on board the *Pandora* and ready for an Arctic cruise !

And now before we start the little vessel from Portsmouth, I will give a list of the officers and men who composed our ship's company.

Captain.

ALLEN WILLIAM YOUNG, Esq., Lieut. R.N.R.

Lieutenants.

F. G. INNES-LILLINGSTON, R.N. (*retired*).

GEORGE PIRIE, R.N.

L. R. KOOLEMANS BEYNEN, Dutch Royal Navy.

Doctor.

ARTHUR HORNER.

Artist.

GEORGE DE WILDE.

Correspondent for New York Herald.

J. MCGAHAN.

Warrant Officers.

HENRY TOMS . . . . Gunner.
HENRY MITCHELL . . Boatswain.
GEORGE BALL . . . . Engineer.
ARTHUR PORTEUS . . Assistant Engineer.
HENRY JAMES . . . . Carpenter.

Crew.

JOSEPH SHELTON . . . Ship's Cook
H. MIHIL . . . . . . Quartermaster.
J. TIMPSON . . . . . Do.
C. TIZZARD . . . . . Boatswain's Mate.
H. ANDREWS . . . . Captain of Tops.
W. RANDERSON . . . Harpooner.
T. FLORENCE . . . . Captain of the Hold.

J. MOTH	Sailmaker.
C. VINE	Captain's Coxswain.
W. PENNINGTON . . .	A.B.
E. GRACE	A.B.
A. GILLES	A.B.
W. DAVIS	A.B.
GEORGE THORNE . .	A.B.
W. EDWARDS	Ship's Steward.
J. LAWRENCE	Wardroom Steward.
ESQUIMAUX JOE . . .	Interpreter.

Pirie was to do the navigating duty, and also any surveying that might have to be done, as well as keep watch; so his hands were pretty full. Beynen kept the morning and 4 to 6 watches every day, as well as keeping a very correct journal for his Minister of Marine. The doctor kept the meteorological journal, and did duty as naturalist, as well as look after the health of the crew; whilst our artist sketched, and

McGahan wrote for the *New York Herald.*
So everybody had their separate duties to
perform, and all had to pull and haul when
requisite.

At 4 P.M on the 26th, the government
tug came alongside to tow our head round,
and as we cast off from her, the crews of
her Majesty's ships honoured us with giving
us their parting cheers. As we passed the
St. Vincent, the boys on board her manned
the rigging, and gave forth three rattling
cheers. All the yachts we passed cheered,
and a band on Southsea Pier struck up,
"Rule, Britannia," and "Home, sweet
home."

We steamed to Cowes, and made fast
to a buoy for the night, with the intention
of an early start the following morning,
on the principle that "Sunday sail never
fail."

At 4 A.M., while all good folks on shore were in bed, we slipped from our buoy, and proceeded under steam through the Solent. It was a lovely summer's morning, with just a nice cool breeze blowing, and everything looked bright and beautiful in the morning sun.

Off Yarmouth, Isle of Wight, we stopped and sent ashore our farewell telegrams to friends and relations, saying that we were fairly off at last, though seven days later than our first intention. Setting our fore and aft sails to a slight breeze from S.S.W., we were soon abreast of Portland.

The ships in Portland, taking us for a man-of-war, had hoisted the "Demand"; so we made our number, to let them know who we were, and the *Warrior* threw out the signal, "Wish you success!" to which we replied, "Thanks!" and "Adieu!"

At 6 P.M. we were able to make all plain sail; but in the first watch a gale of wind sprung up in our teeth, and we had to shorten and furl sail.

A gale of wind in the Channel, on a dark and windy night, with a new crew, is not the pleasantest thing in the world, as the men have not had time to learn where each rope leads to, but it does wonders in the way of shaking them into their places, and teaching them where to find every rope next time. A voice would be heard from the fore topsail yard, hailing the deck, " On deck there !" " Let go your fore topsail buntline !" and a minute or two afterwards the same voice would be heard anathematising a brother shipmate on deck, and singing out, " You've let go the jib halliards instead of the buntline !" &c.

Our Captain was on deck the whole

night, and Pirie took the wheel for several hours ; but towards morning the gale abated, and we steamed into Plymouth harbour, and made fast to a buoy.

As Captain Young had so much to do before starting, he asked Pirie and me to call on Sir Henry Keppel, and apologise to him for his not calling in person. Sir Henry received us most warmly, and said that he wished he was going with us himself. He was most kind, offering us the water-tank to fill up our water-casks, and willing to do anything to help us.

Pirie and I then went and put the finishing touch to our shopping, there being a few little requisites to get before starting. On our return on board, we found Sir Henry, who had come on board in a downpour of rain, to see his friend, our Captain, and to inquire if he could be of any service to him. We also received a parting visit from Lord Mount-Edgcumbe.

In the evening we slipped from the buoy and made our final start for the north. As we passed the breakwater, the keeper of the lighthouse at the end of it gave a wave or two with his cap, and dipped his ensign three times to us, as a signal of " Farewell."

That evening, as we sat round our mess-table over our grog, we drank " Success to the Expedition," but when somebody proposed to drink their health as well, the doctor would not hear of it, as he said if we were all too healthy, his principal occupation would be gone !

On the 29th we spoke a homeward bound merchantman, and asked him to take letters for us. She proved to be the *Queen of Australia*, from Calcutta to

Dundee, and was 125 days out. Her Captain kindly took our letters, and we sent them our latest papers.

That evening we passed the Scilly Islands, stopped our engines, and banked fires.

The next morning we raised our screw, which made a wonderful difference in our sailing; but nothing of importance occurred until July 2nd, when we had to close reef our topsails, as it came on to blow a heavy gale of wind from the north-west. We took a good deal of water in over the bows, as the sea was very heavy, and I fancy the cook must have had some trouble to keep his fire alight, as quantities went down the fore skylight on to his cooking galley, notwithstanding which he managed to give us an uncommonly good roast leg of mutton for dinner.

c

Our meal hours were : breakfast, 8.30
A.M. ; dinner, 1.30 P.M. ; and tea at 6 P.M. ;
but as we got north, we got so hungry
that they were altered to 7.30 for breakfast, and as soon after 12.30 as convenient
to the cook for our dinner.

On the 3rd, we shook out reefs, the
weather having moderated ; and on Sunday,
the 4th, we had light north-westerly winds.

We passed a great many porpoises, and
one large shark that day, or, rather, I
should say that they passed us, as we had
very little wind, whilst they were going
through the water as if they were " making
a passage."

The weather was very warm, and there
was a curious mist hanging about the
horizon, which made us think we were
going to have a change of wind ; but,
alas ! that change did not come for several

days, as the wind remained in the north-west quarter as if nailed there.

By the 6th of July, nine days had passed and gone since we left Cowes, and we were still in the latitude of the Scilly Islands, the wind remaining foul ; and on the 8th it blew a heavy gale from the northward and westward, which lasted until the afternoon of the 9th, on which day we had a very sudden shift of wind early in the morning, which, had it taken us aback, might have proved very serious. In the evening it freshened up again, and a heavy squall coming on carried away our jibboom.

During the night, the wind increased, and in the middle watch we had to turn all hands out to close reef the topsails, and that only just in time, as it came on to blow in very heavy squalls; and by

c 2

breakfast time it was blowing a regular sneezer.

Our Captain scarcely ever left the deck, except to look at the glass and for breakfast; but by noon the weather, though still bad, having become a little more settled, he was able to turn in for a short time, and get some sleep.

Our wheel-ropes, which turned out to be very bad, now showed such serious signs of wearing through that we thought it advisable to reeve new ones.

Towards evening the gale moderated, and by midnight we had only a slight breeze.

Sunday was lovely, and glad we all were to get a sunny day to dry our wet clothes. It also brought us a fair wind, and with squared yards we bowled along gaily; and our evening church service was carried on with some comfort.

Monday still found us with a fair wind, but our little ship rolled tremendously, and our rigging having given out very much in the bad weather we had encountered made us anxious for our masts. We succeeded, however, in setting it up afresh, and kept our fair wind until Thursday, the 5th, when it again shifted to the old quarter, right in our teeth.

How we hated the very mention of a north-west wind, so persistently did it blow, and when it did subside, only left us in what was worse, namely, the "doldrums." To have this weather in the North Atlantic when one expected fine fair south-west winds was enough to try anybody's temper, and we had recourse to various ways of keeping jolly.

Sailors, I am afraid, are rather given to practical jokes, more especially when they can get a landsman on board to play them off upon, and one practical joke which we played upon our good-natured doctor I am tempted to insert here. I hope he will forgive me for publishing it.

As I have before mentioned, he used to keep the meteorological journal, and for the purpose of registering the quantity of ozone in the atmosphere, he had a small box made, with a door opening on hinges, and a lot of holes bored in the side, which he used to hoist to the masthead with a piece of chemically prepared paper in it, which showed by its deepness of colour, every twenty-four hours, the amount of ozone.

One evening, we lowered this box, placed in it a small tobacco-pouch, made in imitation of a grisly bear, with a very fierce expression, and hoisted it again to its former position at the main truck. The next morning our friend and messmate, the doctor, as usual, went to the signal halliards, and lowered his precious box ; but instead of finding his usual piece of paper hanging inside, he met a miniature green-eyed monster staring him full in the face. He dropped the box like a hot potato, and the success of the trick was greeted with roars of laughter from all the witnesses. With such like jokes we used to pass away these tedious hours of monotony in the lone, and

On these calm days we sometimes made up a crew of officers, and would go for a pull in one of our whale-boats, which was better exercise than walking up and down our coal-laden deck ; and in the evening we would occasionally have a friendly round or two with boxing-gloves.

The sea-birds in these parts were uncommonly tame, and would follow us in our boat, or allow us to pull close up to them before attempting to rise. We caught one, a Fulmar petrel, with the intention of keeping it as a pet, but it could not bear captivity, and died, poor thing, before a week was over.

On the morning of the 26th we sighted a three-masted schooner, hull down, on the horizon, and that night, in the middle watch, she came close alongside, and hailed us, asking if we were the *Pandora*.

We answered in the affirmative, and when daylight broke, she signalled to us that she had newspapers on board of July 12th; so we boarded her, and were very kindly received by her Captain. She was the *Traveller*, bound from Peterhead to Ivigtut for cryolite, this being her second voyage this year, she having already taken one cargo to Copenhagen.

She had left Peterhead on the 12th July, and had got as far in fourteen days as we had in thirty, she having experienced strong north-easterly winds, whilst we had nothing but north-westerly winds and calms.

We grumbled very much at our ill luck, and laid it down to the fact of not having a cat on board when we sailed from England.

The Captain of the *Traveller* took letters for us, as he hoped to be home early in September, and saying " Good-bye" to him, we returned on board our own ship, and again making sail, away we stood together for some time; but his ship being light, and ours being heavy, he was soon past us, though some way down to leeward, He told us that there was coal to be had

at Ivigtut should we have to steam before
we got there. We were very glad to
hear this, as our water was not very far
from an end, and should we meet much
ice off Cape Desolation (which we eventually did), we could then use our coal
and steam through it.

On the 28th, we sighted our first icebergs, but they were a very long way off,
and for the greater part of the day only
visible from the masthead. But the next
morning, what a sight! I came on deck
at six o'clock, and thought the little vessel
had taken us into fairyland during the
night! I do not think I have ever witnessed such a beautiful scene. There we
were, sailing through masses of ice, which
assumed the most fantastic forms, sometimes appearing like huge beasts, and at
other times like the most beautiful caverns

from which every minute one almost expected to see issuing forth a fairy queen,
followed by her suite of elves, to prophesy
to us either good or evil fortune. This
ice was without doubt the most beautiful
we saw the whole voyage, and I heard
one officer remark what a lovely dress a
good imitation of it would make for a
young lady in a ball room. I certainly
agree with him, but do not believe that the
most skilful dressmaker could ever make
a dress which would come to anything
approaching such beauty. I believe we
saw every shade of blue that is imaginable,
from the deepest to the lightest, and this,
intermixed with the snowy whiteness of the
different parts of the bergs, had an effect
which I cannot, dare not, attempt to
describe.

We were running with a nice fresh

breeze through all this ice, at the rate of about six or seven knots, each hour making the navigation more difficult as the pieces increased in number, and kept the officer of the watch very much on the *qui vive.*

Towards noon signs of an approaching gale appeared; so we shortened sail by close reefing the fore topsail and reefing the trysails, in case of coming to such thick ice as to cause us to haul to the wind; but later in the afternoon the wind, instead of rising, gradually fell lighter, but as it decreased so did the ice increase, and at last we had our first bump, and soon afterwards the floes got so thickly packed together that, seeing no clear space to steer for, Toms, who was officer of the watch, had to put her at an apparently weak place where two large floes met. We were then going at a fair

Forcing a passage through the Ice.

Page 28.

speed, and the force with which we struck made the little ship tremble and quiver, whilst her masts shook with the shock she received, and she came to a momentary standstill. But it was not for long, as she continued to force her way through, pushing aside these masses like a saucy lassie making her way through a rude crowd.

To add to the beauty of the scenery, the high hills in the vicinity of Cape Desolation towered upwards in their purple grandeur over the large grounded icebergs, which formed a pleasant foreground to this most perfect view.

Before long we sighted a couple of large seals basking in the sun on a flat floepiece; so rifles were got ready, and as soon as we came abreast of them, two or three of us fired, hitting them both.

One however wriggled himself into the
water and disappeared, whilst the other
after a few struggles lay motionless, with
his head close to the edge of the floe and
apparently dead. A boat was immediately manned, and I got into it intending
to bring our prize on board. On nearing
him, he turned out to be a large bladder-
nose seal, and we soon saw that he was
not dead. One of our men (Andrews),
fearing that he would work his way off
the ice, jumped on to it, with the intention
of attacking him in the rear, and by
holding on to his two hind flippers,
which served him for a tail, prevent his
escape, but the moment his extra weight,
added to that of the seal, came upon the
floe, which had been deeply undermined
by the action of the water, a large piece
broke off, throwing him seal and all into

the sea.   The seal disappeared immediately, to be seen no more, whilst we got
Andrews into the boat, rather cold, but
none the worse for his ducking. I felt very
small on returning on board again without
what appeared to everybody a certain prize,
and you may be sure our shipmates had
a good laugh at us for having lost it.

We sighted a great many more that
afternoon, but as our time was too precious
to go after those a long way off, we had
to content ourselves by doing our best
to shoot those which we happened to pass
close to *en route.*

We soon sighted another fine big fellow
a little on the lee bow, and as all hands
had now got rifles, some very rapid and
independent firing was kept up. He did
not quite seem to understand the whizzing
of the "Snider" bullets which struck the

ice all round him, and seemed undecided
on which side of the floe to take the water,
as he first wriggled himself one way and
then the other; but at last his head fell,
and he lay motionless. We all thought
he had been mortally hit, so a boat was
lowered and sent to bring him on board;
but on the boat nearing the floe, he again
showed signs of life, so someone fired from
the boat, and then for the first time we
saw blood. They soon pulled alongside
the ice, and Beynen despatched him with
a shot from his Snider.

Strange to relate, no one had hit him
from the ship! What bad shots we must
all have made! He was soon skinned,
cut up, and hung in our rigging, and we
looked forward to having some real fresh
meat for breakfast next morning instead of
preserved provisions.

The wind having now fallen light, Captain Young ordered steam to be got up, and, furling sails, we commenced threading our way under its propelling power through innumerable and thickly packed floe pieces of Spitzbergen ice. This Spitzbergen ice is quite different to that which is met with in Melville Bay and the northern parts of Baffin Bay, it having been subjected to the action of the waves for many months during its drift down the east coast of Greenland, and here, where it is carried up by a northerly current after having rounded Cape Farewell, it is broken into many pieces, most of which, however, are of considerable area.

This ice is much dreaded by all whalers going northward, and they generally keep well to the west of it if possible, running

D

between it and the main pack which drifts down Davis Straits. The ships which go to Ivigtut for cryolite have nearly always to contend with it before getting into that port.

Late in the evening we sighted five large seals lying on the ice close together; so we neared them, and managed to get two out of the five, one, a wounded one, effecting his escape, and I do not believe that anybody aimed at the remaining two, who quickly took to the water. However, two were better than none, and we soon had a boat down and went after them. These animals are very quick at getting into the water, unless hit fair in the head, and both of those we secured had managed to get off the ice; but a shot through the head settled one whilst in the act of diving, and the other, finding himself too hard hit to swim, clambered up again, and another bullet soon terminated his miseries.

Whilst some of the party were getting our prey into the boat, others were taking a cruise across the floe, hoping peradventure there might be another seal lying on the opposite side; but none were to be seen. However, they discovered some pools of fresh water, which to all hands was a most acceptable discovery, as we had been on an allowance for some time. The ship was brought alongside the floe, and secured to it by laying out two ice-anchors, and then commenced the work of watering ship by buckets full. Whilst the ship was being brought alongside, two of our officers amused themselves by climbing to the top of a hummock, and sliding down one of its sloping sides, much to the detriment of

their tailor's cloth, neither of them wearing, like Pat Haggarty, a pair of "old
leather breeches!" Two pools being
close together, officers and men all set to
work filling and carrying buckets to the
ship, the party belonging to each pool
vying with one another who would send
the greatest number on board. It was
about 9.30 P.M. when we commenced this
work, and about ten the sun was just
setting, throwing a rich purple glow over
the whole of the ice around us, and
making the scene most picturesque.

It was not long before we had sufficient
water on board to last us for some time;
so, scrambling into the old ship again, we
cast off and stood on once more towards
the land. Next morning finding us abreast
of the entrance to the Arsuk Fiord, Captain Young determined to enter it and lay

in a fresh stock of coal at Ivigtut, a small
Danish settlement lying about sixteen
miles up the fiord.

Off the entrance we were rather sur-
prised to see a vessel under sail and
battling with the ice, which here was
very thickly collected, and still more sur-
prised were we when, on nearing her, she
proved to be our old friend the *Traveller*.
She was almost becalmed, having nothing
but baffling flaws of light air off the land ;
so Captain Young offered to tow her in,
an offer which her Captain gladly accepted,
he himself coming on board us to act as
pilot. We did not arrive off the settlement until the evening, when, our Captain
having been on shore and ascertained for
certain that we could get coal here, we
were soon lashed alongside the barque

Thor, which saved us having to let go
our anchor in thirty fathoms of water.

We were immediately boarded by thou-
sands of mosquitoes, which nearly drove
all hands mad. They were the largest I
have ever seen.

The engineer of the mines here kindly
gave us a gang of men to coal our ship,
so we were able to give most of our own
men a little leave to run on shore. The
party coaling us worked with gauze bags
over their heads as a protection against
the mosquitoes.

As I have before mentioned, this is a
Danish settlement consisting of a few
houses occupied by the head men of the
place, and some smaller ones occupied by
the labourers who come from Denmark to
work in the cryolite mines. These mines

are in appearance more like quarries, and cryolite is a very valuable mineral, containing a great deal of aluminum and fluate of soda.

The doctor of the settlement kindly invited us up to his house, and we spent a very pleasant evening there, and afterwards paid a visit to the head man of the place, who is there to see that the proper royalty is paid to the Danish government by the company that works their mines. He had a bowl of punch prepared for us, and received us most hospitably.

Between our visits Pirie and I went to visit the cemetery, to which one's attention is attracted by a large white cross on the top of a small hill above the town. We walked up there with one of the Danes, and on our arrival we found another white cross, which served as a monument for all those buried there, and on which was an inscription taken from the 139th Psalm—

" If I take the wings of the morning, and dwell in the uttermost parts of the sea; even there shall Thy hand lead me, and Thy right hand shall hold me."

One could not but feel sad, looking on the graves of those who had left their homes to come and die in this desolate spot; but it was a consolation to know that many were those of Esquimaux who had been converted to Christianity by the never tiring exertions of the good Moravian missionaries.

The ground here is hard rock; so they cannot dig graves, but build up stones round the bodies, and cover them with mould, each grave looking like a small garden plot on a raised terrace.

In the harbour lay the renowned little *Fox*, which Sir Leopold M'Clintock commanded on her eventful cruise to these waters, and in which our Captain had also served with him, as well as Toms, our gunner, and Florence, our captain of the hold. Captain Young had also commanded her on another expedition to Greenland, when there were thoughts of laying the Atlantic cable by the Faroe Isles to Cape Farewell, and so to Newfoundland.

We sent a mail bag from here by the *Traveller*, as she expected to be home early in September.

At 3 A.M. the next morning we cast off and stood out of the harbour, having got a good supply of coal on board. But what a state the ship was in. The coal was "North Country" coal, and conse-

quently dreadfully black and dusty, and
the dew in the night had turned the
dust into black mud. Everything was
covered with it, and we all looked like
coal heavers walking about the deck.

I forgot to mention that our men on
landing had immediately commenced a
search, in hopes of finding a cat, and as
everyone went on their own hunting-
grounds, they returned with three cats
and a young pig. One of these cats soon
afterwards presented the ship's company
with five kittens, so we certainly made
up for our oversight in leaving England
without a pussy. Our pig was a most
extraordinary feeder. It would leave good
potato pealings and messes brought up to
it from the lower deck to go and have
a substantial meal on coals! I have seen
him crunching away at the above men-

tioned mineral and enjoying it, his little corkscrew tail waggling round and round with delight, whilst he would occasionally give a grunt which sounded as if he was gratified to the highest degree of gratification. Can naturalists explain why he should so relish coal? Was it because his system in that climate required a diet of carbon, or was it simply a piggish idea of his own? He was white when he arrived on board, but soon afterwards changed his colour for that of his favourite food, and did not return to his natural state until all coal was off the upper deck and he had had two or three good " dousings " from the hose when washing decks in the morning.

But we must leave " Dennis," as our men had named him, to himself, and return to our ship. After leaving the Arsuk

Fiord, we shaped a course to the northward, having still a good deal of ice to thread our way through; but we hugged the land now, leaving the thickest of the ice out to seaward of us. Having a fair wind, we made sail, and so under steam and sail we went a tolerable pace; but in the afternoen we had again to furl sails, and at ten o'clock that night we had got amongst such very thick ice that we had to steam very slowly, and it was so dark that we could not make out the floe pieces until they were close under the bows, the consequence being that we got several very severe bumps, and at last had to stop the engines altogether. Some time after midnight however, whilst lying in my bed, I heard the screw commence again; so I presumed that it had got lighter, and I was soon asleep, waking next morning to find a very wet day had set in. However, with the rain came a fair wind; so banking our fires again, we made sail to it. Divine service was performed in the evening instead of the morning, which our Captain afterwards made the regular rule, as it gave those who had been on deck nearly all night some time longer to sleep. The next day was also wet and foggy, but our fair wind had failed us; so furling sails, we once more drew our fires forward, and, getting our "tail tickler" under way, proceeded under steam alone. We passed several solitary bergs, but nothing of any importance occurred that day. Next morning, the fog having lifted, we observed land on the starboard beam, bearing east by south; and thinking we might be over one of the Torske banks, we sounded, but found no bottom at seventy fathoms. A

light southerly wind now springing up,
it was " Make sail ! " again, " Stop steaming ! " but towards evening it again fell
calm, so we once more furled sails. At
11 P.M. the sun could not have been very
far below the horizon, as there was a
bright red glow away to the northward,
like what one sees about half an hour after
an English sunset. Of course it was perfect daylight.

I find that I have got Wednesday, the
4th, down in my journal as " A beautiful
" bright clear morning, like a fine frosty
" English winter day, but the sun quite
" warm. The land clear and close to on the
" starboard hand. Such scenery I never
" saw before. The wildest and most rugged
" rocks, of a neutral tint, towering above
" the sea, with occasionally a glimpse of a
" fiord showing miles inland, and still chain

" after chain of high volcanic mountains,
" but not one sign of vegetation to relieve
" the eye."

The little *Pandora* disappointed us very
much with regard to her rate of steaming,
but I think a good deal of it was owing
to her bottom having got so foul during
the calms she had in the Atlantic. The
weeds were now several inches in length,
and as we looked over the side, we could
see them aggravatingly waving about in
the water as they rose and fell with the
slight roll of the ship.

Towards noon we sighted breakers running some little way out from the land,
and therefore altered course to clear them;
but whilst we were at dinner, she struck,
bumped, and off again. We all jumped on
deck, and found that though well clear
of the breakers and apparently in deep

water, we had passed over a rock outside
of them with a touch-and-go. These rocks,
not being down on the chart, form our first
discovery, and the Captain has given them
the name of "Pandora's Reef." Their
latitude is 66° 11' N., and their longitude
53° 45' W.

In the evening three kyaks were observed coming out from the land ; so we
stopped and waited for them, hoisting each
of them inboard as they arrived alongside.
This was done by passing a rope under
the bow and another under the stern, the
occupant remaining seated in the middle
until canoe and all were hoisted level with
the bulwarks, when he got out, and the
kyak was lifted inboard.

These natives were intelligent, good-
natured-looking fellows, and two out of
the three were a very fair size ; but the

third was a mite, though I think he must have been the eldest. They grinned and chattered away to their hearts' content, but of course we could not understand each other till we got Esquimaux Joe aft. They each had five very fine salmon trout tucked under the sealskin lines which are stretched across the tops of their kyaks, and also some dried salmon stowed away underneath. These kyaks are formed by, first of all, a framework of wood being built in the shape they require, and then sealskin, properly prepared, is stretched over it, the seams being beautifully sewn together and made watertight by being smeared with some composition, the only aperture being a round hole in the centre in which the occupant sits.

The lower edge of the jumper worn by the natives exactly fits over this hole, the

E

elasticity of the skin of which it is composed causing it to contract underneath a small rim of wood, thus rendering the whole canoe perfectly watertight.

Their implements for hunting are most beautifully made. They generally carry two spears, one for seals and the other for fish. The seal spears are formed of wood and ivory (or bone), the shaft being wood and the head ivory. One end of a long line of sealskin is secured to the head, which disconnects from the shaft on entering the seal's flesh, the other end being attached to a large " drogue," or inflated skin, so that any attempt to escape by diving on the part of the animal that has been struck is frustrated by the " drogue," which, acting as a buoy, he is unable to drag under water. The wooden shaft, becoming disconnected, floats, and is easily

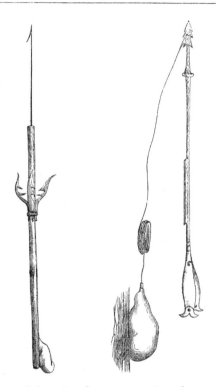

recovered by the hunter. At the opposite end of the shaft are two ornamentally shaped, flat, broad pieces of ivory, which

E 2

do the same duty for the spear that
feathers do for an arrow. The fish spear
is a most ingenious contrivance. The shaft
is of wood, not very long, and the head
is nothing but a long sharp iron spike,
with only one barb; but about a third of
the way up the shaft are three pieces of
curved bone, each with two barbs on the
inner side, lashed to the wood in such a
manner that, should the iron spike miss
the fish, he is pretty nearly sure to get
jammed between the pieces of bone. An
inflated bladder at the other end acts in
lieu of the above mentioned flat pieces of
ivory, which they use on their larger
spears. It also keeps the spear from sink-
ing, should the iron point be too heavy for
the wood to float.

Their paddles, which are also very
neatly made, have a blade at each end,

shaped the same way as the blades of English oars; but the ends are tipped with bone, and a thin rim of the same substance runs along the edges of each blade.

But whilst giving all these descriptions, I have forgotten our interesting visitors, whom we left on the quarterdeck, having just hoisted them on board; so I will now return to them.

One by one we took them below, and, giving them each a pipe of tobacco to smoke, which they seemed to enjoy very much, asked them different questions.

We, however, did not get much out of them, and all we heard was that " One big ship been along coast buy dogs." We conjectured that this was the *Valorous.*

We bought their fish from them, giving them a biscuit apiece for each fish, and a small quantity of tobacco. Our men also made them a present of tobacco, which tells well for the generosity of the British sailor.

Our time however was precious, and we could delay the ship no longer; so saying good bye to our new acquaintances, and lowering them over the side in the same way in which we had hoisted them on board, we made preparations for continuing our voyage. As each was lowered, he shook hands with us, and on their all three being once more on the water, they gave us a cheer, English fashion, and paddled for the shore as if they were racing. We then proceeded under steam once more, and were soon enveloped in a dense fog.

When these natives were on board, Captain Young had asked one what he would do should a fog come on, or should it come

on to blow a gale of wind, and they so far
from shore. He only laughed, and said
they would go anywhere in their kyaks.
It is related of one man that he actually
went from Greenland to Iceland in his
kyak, being five days at sea. He did not
do it intentionally, but was blown away
from the coast in a westerly gale, and all
he could do was to paddle his canoe before
the wind to prevent her capsizing. For
five days and nights he held on his course,
and though he had food and water in his
canoe, he could not get at it, as it was
stowed underneath the sealskin deck, and
not attainable without his first getting out
of the kyak himself, which of course he
could not do at sea. He was eventually
picked up by a Danish ship close to the
coast of Iceland, and thus saved.

The fog we had run into cleared away

before the morning watch, and left us a
bright and clear sunny day, with a good
breeze, which helped us along gaily, and
making sail once more, we stopped our
engines. That morning we had some of
the salmon trout for breakfast, and only
those who have been a long time without
really fresh food can well understand how
we enjoyed them.

CHAPTER II.

THE FAR NORTH.

" And now there came both mist and snow,
  And it grew wondrous cold ;
  And ice mast-high came floating by
  As green as emerald."—*Coleridge.*

ON the morning of the 7th we arrived off the island of Discoe, and Mr. Elberg, the governor, kindly came out to meet us, and brought a pilot with him. He informed us that the government expedition had sailed ten days previously for the Waigat Channel to fill up with coal, and that the *Valorous* had returned home on the same day ; so our hopes of being able to give them their letters fell to the ground.

We were soon anchored safely in the little harbour called Godhavn, on the shores of which is situated the Danish settlement of Lievely ; but as it was very early in the morning, we none of us landed at once, but lay down and had a couple of hours' rest.

After breakfast we commenced the work of watering ship, this being accomplished by our boats towing our water casks on shore, filling them at a stream which lay some way from the ship, and then towing them on board again, and pumping them out when alongside. Whilst this was going on, several of us went on shore, the doctor to shoot, our artist to take sketches and photographs, and Pirie and Beynen to take observations for finding the error and rate of our chronometers. I landed later and tried to get some dogs, but the *Alert* and *Discovery* had bought nearly everything that was to be bought, not only dogs, but all the skins and fur clothing that the natives could spare. I managed however to purchase a kyak, which I hoped I might find useful in the North, and even should it not prove so (which it did not), it would at any rate be a capital curiosity to take home.

Mr. Elberg treated us with great kindness and hospitality, and informed us that as it was always the custom of the young ladies of Lievely to give a dance to every ship that came in, they had sent to ask if Captain Young would allow the men to come on shore that evening to a ball which it was their intention to give.

We went to see the room in which the said ball was to come off. It was a cooper's shed of not very large dimensions, and very dark; and on entering I found that I could not quite stand upright in it; so it did not promise well for dancing. Above the door we found an inscription written, evidently left there by some blue-jacket belonging to the other ships. It ran as follows :—

" Musichall dore open this evenin 8 clock."

After our visit to this " Hall of dazzling light " (?), some of us invested in a few things from the Danish store, such as needles, pigtail tobacco, &c., with the hope of being able to exchange them for curiosities, should we happen to fall in with any uncivilised natives further north. A few detached wooden houses, a wooden-built church and school, compose the principal part of the town, the remainder consisting of native huts made of turf; the governor's house being conspicuous, and having a

DORE OPEN THIS EVENING 8.OCLOCK

Entrance to the Ball Room at Disco.

Page 60.

battery in front and a flag-staff, from which floated the Danish flag.

In the afternoon Mr. Elberg and Mr. Fenker, who was to relieve him and become future governor, paid us a visit, and after the work of watering was completed, we gave the crew leave to have a run on shore.

The ball that night was well attended both by the Discoe belles as well as the *Pandora's* crew; in fact, the room was so crowded and oppressive that everybody agreed it would be better to finish the dancing outside; and as it was broad daylight all night, there was no occasion for illuminations of any kind. The boat was to come ashore for everybody at 11 P.M., so that we might get on board and up anchor before midnight. Accordingly, at the appointed hour, we all went down to

the beach after having said good bye to
our dusky partners, who, by the bye, dance
uncommonly well ; but though we had
taken farewell of them, they followed us
down to the boat, and after we had shoved
off, set up a low wail, which gradually
grew into a howl, in which all the dogs
joined. We took this as a parting com-
pliment, though I cannot say it was particularly musical.

I think here that I must try and give a
short description of these young ladies'
dresses, which to them are certainly very
becoming. Their hair is all brushed up
to the top of the head, terminating in a
curious sort of topknot, tied with either
red, green, or blue ribbon, a handkerchief
of the same colour being bound round the
head just over the forehead. Their upper
garment is what a sailor would call a loose

You truck 'em?

Page 63.

"jumper," which reaches as far as the waist, with a neat frill round the neck, the continuation to this being (pray, don't be shocked, lady reader) *sealskin breeches,* tucked into neatly fitting long boots, which cover the knee, and are either a brilliant red or yellow colour, with a white stripe down the front. The novelty and convenience of dancing with young ladies unencumbered with long skirts or heavy trains was greatly appreciated by all of us.

Several of these young ladies had different curiosities for sale or barter, and would waylay us outside the door and try and tempt us to buy sealskin purses or slippers, and various other badly made and worthless articles. When they wanted you to buy or barter, they simply held out the article, and said, in an interrogating manner, " You truck 'em ? " One young woman came up to me holding out an attempt at an imitation of an English muff, and looking up in my face with what, I suppose, she considered a very winning smile (she was dreadfully ugly), asked me if I would " truck 'em." I said, " What have you got there ? " and Captain Young, who was standing behind her, much to her astonishment answered for her by simply saying, " Only some rubbish ! "

Turning round on him, she stamped her foot with rage (the winning smile was no longer there, and her expression now wore an ugly frown), and mustering all the English she knew, she at the top of her voice shrieked out to him, " What you say, Cap'n ? " " What you tell 'em, Cap'n ? " " What you speak 'em, Cap'n ? " each question being enforced by a stamp from her little foot. Her rage was too ridiculous, and I burst out laughing, as also did one of her own countrywomen, who was standing close to and listening. This was the climax. She could stand it no longer, and, turning her back to us, ran off to hide her anger.

The moment we got on board, the anchor was weighed, and we steamed out of this snug little nook, shaping a course along the land towards the Waigat Channel, where we heard that there was coal which Captain Nares, R.N., had kindly ordered to be dug out in readiness for us on our arrival. The whole of the next day we were steaming through the southern portion of this channel amongst innumerable icebergs, which were constantly breaking up or rolling over, the noise caused by them being like that of heavy artillery, which continued day and night without ceasing.

The whole scene was very grand, and

F

there was something very awe-inspiring
in the continued thunder (if I may use the
word) caused by the breaking-up of these
huge masses of ice. At midnight it came
on very thick, and as we were close to
land, and surrounded by bergs, our Captain
decided to make the ship fast to one lying
just ahead of us, and which he conjectured
from its size to be aground. We accordingly laid out two ice-anchors, a task not
always unattended with danger, as sometimes a blow from a pickaxe will result
in the splitting off of a large piece of the
berg, on which one or more men may
happen to be standing, thus endangering
their lives, as well as the lives of those in
the boat carrying the hawser. We were
rather amused at the cautious manner in
which our harpooner used his pickaxe;
he once before, whilst serving in a whale-

ship, having had a narrow escape when performing the same duty; and his careful movements reminded us of the old saying, "Once bit, twice shy."

The fog was now so dense that we could scarcely see the berg to which we were made fast, and knowing how many other bergs were round us, we congratulated ourselves upon having attained a comparatively safe position. A look-out was placed to keep watch on the hawsers, and the remainder of the watch were sent below. They had not, however, been down many minutes when, with a loud crack, the berg canted towards us, taking the two ice-anchors under water. Fortunately for us, it did not turn completely over; had it done so, it might have fared badly with our little ship. Shortly afterwards, our two anchors having lost their hold, we again resumed our voyage, and the fog having partially cleared, we were enabled to see far enough ahead to steer clear of these ugly customers.

During the whole of the next day, however, we had thick weather, and consequently passed, unknowingly, the village for which we were looking; we were therefore, subjected to the annoyance of retracing our course for some distance. On arriving off the village, which rejoices in the name of Uryarasusuk, Captain Young and myself landed, and were received on the beach by the head man, a Dane, who informed us that there were sixteen men and six women waiting for us at the coaling-place, who would assist us in digging and in loading our boats. We purchased four dogs, which we selected from a large number that had congregated round us, and returned on board, followed shortly afterwards by the governor, who brought the dogs we had purchased on board with him, and went with us some way towards the Kudliset coal cliffs. After proceeding a short distance, we met a small sloop, which we found contained the very people who were to assist us in coaling. Calling her alongside, the governor ordered them to proceed with us, he himself returning home in the sloop.

On our arrival at the coaling-place, we anchored, intending to commence coaling early in the morning. Besides our own crew, we now had on board ten or twelve men and five women (four young ladies and their duenna), and the question arose as to where we should place our female visitors for the night. This difficulty, however, was soon overcome by our wrapping them up, chaperone and all, in a big sail, on the floor of the chart-room.

All hands were turned out the next morning at 4.30, and after breakfast, steam having been got up in our steam-launch, the work of coaling commenced. Two-thirds of the ship's company were landed, with all the natives, for the purpose of filling the coal-bags; but our disappointment was great on finding that no coal had been dug at the place to which they led us. There was nothing for it but to set to work with pick and shovel, and dig for ourselves. This coal lies in seams, running horizontally along the face of the cliff, and the one from which we commenced taking our coal lay about sixty or seventy feet above the level of the sea at the top of a slope formed by loose sandstone which had fallen from the cliff

above. Down this slope the blocks of
coal were rolled as they were dug out,
the women and two or three men filling
the bags on the beach, and carrying them
to the boats, which, as fast as they were
loaded, were towed alongside the ship by
the steam-launch. Every one took his turn
at digging, officer as well as man, and
by dinner time I think everybody was
ravenous, this exercise proving very con-
ducive to a good appetite. I cannot speak
too highly in praise of the energy and
industry displayed by the women. These
Arctic *belles* chatted and worked away in
the most cheerful and good-natured manner,
and certainly assisted us more than the
men of their party. It was amusing to
notice the vanity of woman exhibiting
itself even in these simple people; evi-
dences. were not wanting that our fair

young coal-diggers were as subject to this failing as the more civilised of their sex. Three times during the day—the white linen tops of their boots having got soiled with coal-dust—they ran away to their boat and changed them. I think that all the young ladies of the island of Disco are very particular in keeping this article of dress spotlessly clean.

At noon, the general recall was seen flying from our mast-head; so we all repaired on board to dinner, after which we resumed our work, but had not been very long at it, when McGahan, who had wandered some distance along the beach, returned to us with the news that he had found a quantity of coal which had been dug out and was ready for shipping   This, no doubt, was the coal which Captain Nares had ordered to be dug for us. Why the "huskies" did not take us to this seam at first, we could not understand. We did not finish work till past six that evening, and, on returning on board, found that we had managed to ship, in twelve hours, forty tons of coal, which, considering that we had to dig a good deal of it ourselves, we thought very satisfactory work.

Captain Young ordered some food to be given to the natives who had been working for us, and we invited the women of the party to come down and take tea with us. They did not, at first, seem quite to understand the art of using a knife and fork, but soon mastered this accomplishment. After tea they sang some of their native songs, one of the girls playing an accompaniment on the concertina. It was now getting late, and they wished to start for Uryara-susuk; so, taking leave of us, they got into their boats, and, giving us a farewell cheer, shoved off, and were soon out of sight.

Early the next morning we were once more under weigh, and steamed out of the Waigat, through an immense number of icebergs, which still kept up their thunder all round us. After leaving Waigat Strait, we bore away to the northward, arriving at the settlement of Upernivik on Friday, the 13th of August. We went into the harbour, but did not anchor, as a light southerly breeze was blowing, and we were very anxious to avail ourselves of it. The governor, however, came off to us, and took charge of our letters, which he promised to send home by the next Danish vessel leaving that port. We got two more dogs here, which increased our team to the number of six. By this time the first four had got names; the oldest, having shown himself to be the king, was called "King"; the next was dubbed "Snarlyow," or the "Dog Fiend," he being very fond of showing his teeth, and being quite black, with reddish eyes, had a most diabolical expression. The two younger ones, which were apparently of the same age, and were so like each other that I think they must have been brothers, were called respectively "Starboard" and "Port," from the fact that Starboard always curled up his tail to the right and Port to the left side. Unless they had their tails cocked, it was very hard to tell which was which. Our two new purchases were not long nameless; one, being a lady dog, but apparently very old, was called "Old Mother Grimes," and our men bestowed the name of "Dublin" upon her mate. One of the

men informed us that the latter designation
was decided upon because the dog looked
so like an Irishman.

On leaving the harbour, we found that
the southerly wind had considerably freshened; so, taking a single reef in our topsails, we hoisted them to the "chanty"
of—

"Boney was a warrior,"

and were once more bowling along towards the North, without needing the
assistance of our steam. But this pleasure
was not to last long; the next morning
we again found ourselves in a calm, and
were obliged to have recourse to our kettle
once more. On this day we passed some
of the largest icebergs seen during the
whole voyage, and also had our first fall
of snow. The thermometer on deck showed
35° Fahrenheit. In the evening, a light

wind having sprung up from the westward, we were again able to bank our fires and economise our fuel; the breeze, however, only lasted for the night. This alternation of breeze and calm continued almost throughout the entire outward voyage. On Sunday, the 15th, having exhausted our stock of fresh water, we stopped, and lowered a boat, in order to collect floating fragments of ice, which, after having been allowed to remain in the boat for a few hours, until all salt water had drained from them, were hoisted on board, and soon converted into the most delicious drinking-water. The men used to call this " picking up bits of water." The next evening, whilst at tea, we were startled by the cry of " A bear alongside!"—upon which we deserted the tea-table, and were soon on deck with our rifles. A boat was

quickly manned, and Captain Young and
myself getting into her, we gave chase to
Bruin, who showed himself to be a first-
rate swimmer, and gave our men an uncommonly tough pull. On nearing him,
Captain Young gave him a shot from his
Snider, which penetrated his neck, but did
not stop him, so I tried my *Express*, and
was fortunate enough to hit him in the
head, and he rolled over, quite dead. He
was not a very large bear, but had a very
good coat, which I now possess in the
shape of a handsome rug. This occurred
about fifteen miles from land; so we
imagined that he had been carried away on
some floe of ice, which, having broken up,
left him no alternative but to make for the
land. These animals can live for a long
time swimming in the water, the thick
coating of blubber which lies between

their hides and their flesh keeping them warm, and no doubt acting as nourishment to them when they are a long time without food.

That night, or I should rather say early the next day, it being in the middle-watch, we got into the loose ice at the edge of the pack, during a thick fog, but fortunately were able to steam out of it, though the fog lasted all night. This, however, was an anxious time, as, at just about the same place, and in the latter part of the same month, eighteen years ago, the little *Fox*, commanded by Captain (now Admiral) Sir Leopold M'Clintock, got beset in this pack, and did not break out until the 26th of April in the following year, when, after drifting about 700 miles to the southward, she gallantly made a fresh start, and though a second time caught in the Mel-

ville Bay ice, after battling with it for
many days, and once getting very severely
nipped, got· clear on the 2nd July 1858,
and was at last able to stand to the westward.

We were here surrounded by flocks of
"rotches" (little auks), which used to
settle in companies of about a dozen at a
time on fragments of ice; so Pirie went
away in the dingy, and shot several of
them. He might have got a great many
more if it had not been for the fog, which
was so dense that his distance from the
ship was limited to a few yards, and he
would have been in danger of being lost
altogether had he allowed himself to get
out of sight of her. I should mention
that our engines were stopped, and we
were lying in a dead calm, surrounded by
quantities of small pieces of ice, and only

waiting for the fog to lift to be enabled to proceed. I had the morning watch that morning, and thought I would follow Pirie's good example by going away in the dingy, and getting a few more "rotches" to add to our stock of fresh provisions. I managed to shoot a few, but found it very cold work to pick the dead ones out of the water, the thermometer being down to 27°, and I returned on board very shortly, when Beynen took my place in the boat, and killed several more.

Before breakfast, the fog cleared away; so calling the dingy alongside, we once more began to make progress. That forenoon we passed Cape York, but there was a good deal of ice between us and the land, which prevented our going in and communicating with the natives; and as these curious people have no boats, nor even

G

kyaks, of course they could not come out to us. These natives are completely cut off from intercourse with the outer world, both north and south, by two enormous glaciers, and until Sir John Ross visited them, they imagined themselves to be the only people in existence. They are supposed to be the only tribe on record who, living on the sea-shore, have nothing in the shape of a boat or canoe. Hans, who was with Dr. Kane, was once left there with his kyak, but it is said that hunger compelled them to eat it, or rather, I should say, to eat the sealskin which covered its framework.

We steamed along the edge of the ice, but, on getting farther north, found it stretching away to the westward, and we were therefore compelled to steam for some hours in that direction, though we could

see open water on the other side of it;
but at last, finding a weak place, we
forced the ship through, and were soon
in clear water, and enabled to shape a
direct course for the Carey Islands, which
we sighted the next morning, but did not
arrive at till six o'clock in the evening.

We stopped off the north-west island,
having sighted a cairn on the highest part
of it; and having headed up in casks all
the letters and despatches for her Majesty's
ships *Alert* and *Discovery*, we put them in
a boat, in which the Captain and several
of us started with the view of depositing
them on shore, and hoping also to find
the latest news of those ships, this being
the island on which it was understood
they were to leave a record for us to
take home. We landed at the foot of a
deep gulley, which had evidently been

formed some ages ago by a glacier,
and which was paved, as it were, with
boulders and large loose stones. Leaving
our two casks on the beach, and sending
the boat round to a safer place, we commenced the ascent to the cairn, on reaching which, to our intense surprise, we
could not find a single trace of the expedition—all we discovered being a tin
containing a whaler's record, and a small
bottle of rum, which had been left here in
1867 by some generous hand for the benefit
of future visitors, and which proved very
acceptable, as it was bitterly cold on this
bleak and elevated spot. Farther on, on
a lower elevation, was seen another cairn,
which Beynen started off to examine,
finding, however, nothing but an empty
tin, which must have been left there many
years ago, and on which the names *Reso-*

lute and *Assistance* could be with difficulty deciphered. The question now arose as to what could have happened to the expedition. Had they passed these islands in a fog, or a gale of wind, or had they, like the little *Fox*, got beset in the middle ice, or could they have left their record on another island? We conjectured the former; and as it had come on to blow a gale of wind from the north, we could not, even had there been time, have searched the other islands. Had Captain Young positively known that they had gone on, he says he would have worked up to Littleton Island with their letters; but in the face of a northerly gale, and the season fast passing away, and there being no information as to where the *Alert* and *Discovery* had gone, he considered it best to leave things as they were, and

to proceed on our own affairs ; as, if it
were by any chance possible that the ships
were still south of us, they would pick up
their letters on their way, and, if north,
would probably send down for them in
the spring.

Captain Young wrote a letter to Captain
Nares, explaining the position of our post-
office, and I took this opportunity to scrib-
ble a few lines to my old shipmate, Lieutenant May, of the *Alert.* Putting these
two letters in a tin, we carefully buried
them, and it being now past midnight, we
retraced our steps towards the boat. We
had not gone very far before we arrived at
the top of a very steep slope of snow,
down which we all had to go. Our
different. modes of descent were rather
amusing. Some soberly and discreetly
walked down, each step they took being

deep into the snow; one tried to run down, but overbalancing himself, he finished by rolling till he almost reached the bottom, happily without any injury; whilst others, like our friends on the floe, which I have before mentioned, tried the texture of their *tailor's* cloth. I myself was fortunate enough to be carrying a shovel; so, sitting on it, with the handle to the front, like a witch riding on a broomstick, I slid gaily to the bottom, the shovel forming, as I thought, a novel kind of sledge; but since my arrival in England, I have heard that Commander Cheyne had also used a shovel as a sledge, but for a different purpose, he having dragged on the same kind of implement, for *sixty miles*, the head of a musk-ox. On getting to the beach, we put the casks of letters into a safe position, and erecting a small cairn, stuck a boat-stretcher into the top of it, on which we tied a pocket-handkerchief, and embarking in the boat, we started for the ship.

Though it was past midnight, the sun was shining in the north, causing McGahan, as he pointed first towards it and then to the moon which was shining above our heads, to quote the following lines out of that charming little book, 'Through the Looking-glass' :—

> " The sun was shining on the sea,
>   Shining with all his might ;
>   He did his very best to make
>   The billows smooth and bright ;
>   And this was odd, because it was
>   The middle of the night.
>
> " The moon was shining sulkily,
>   Because she thought the sun
>   Had got no business to be there
>   After the day was done ;
>   ' It's very rude of him,' she said,
>   ' To come and spoil the fun.' "

CHAPTER III.

" WESTWARD HO!"

" The fair breeze blew, the white foam flew,
    The furrow follow'd free;
    We were the first that ever burst
    Into that silent sea."—*Coleridge.*

OUR boat having been hoisted up, we now
bore away for Lancaster Sound, with a
fine breeze after us; but before turning
in, being very hungry, we had each a big
basin of soup, which warmed us up after
our cold expedition to the cairn. Nothing
of importance occurred the next day, but
early in the morning of the 20th we once
more sighted thick ice ahead, and our old
evil genius seemed still to attend us, as no

sooner had we got close to it than down came a thick fog, utterly obscuring it from our sight. We had, of course, to haul to the wind, and as we could best judge, sail along the edge. In the afternoon, however, the fog lifted, and whilst our boat was away getting some more "bits" of water, three bears were sighted not far off, swimming about; so the boat was immediately recalled, and Captain Young, Pirie, Beynen, and McGahan, jumping into her, gave chase. Captain Young and Pirie each managed to shoot one, and, getting close to the third, which was a large cub, Pirie, in a very plucky manner, lassoed him. He immediately got his paws on the gunnel of the boat, and tried to clamber on board her, but with a couple of dexterous kicks, Pirie knocked them off, and making the line fast astern, he was soon

towed alongside, and tethered to the ship.
The boat then went in search of the two
which had been killed, and after finding
them, towed them alongside. Our live
friend was swimming about at the extreme
end of his tether, not a very long one,
and he kept on trying to scramble up the
side, which we were rather glad of, as it
helped to tire him out, and the sooner he
was tired out the better for us, before we
got him on board. Poor little beast! He
looked with wistful eyes at the dead bodies
of his mother and little sister, as they were
being hoisted in. The next job was to get
the little animal himself in. He, though
not so big as his mother, being alive, gave
us more trouble, which, however, we soon
overcame by passing the end of the rope
which was round his neck through a ring-
bolt, and clapping two or three hands on

to it, we hauled his head close down, thus rendering him incapable of biting anybody. Then passing a lashing round his hind legs, we were enabled to make fast a chain round his body, and, as " Jack " would say, " moor him on our quarter-deck." He did not at all seem to like his captivity, and roared in a most angry manner; but his mother having now been skinned, we gave him her skin to lie on, as well as a little bit of her to eat, which he seemed to relish immensely, and as long as he had plenty of her flesh to eat, he remained quiet; but the moment he had finished his repast, he began tearing at her skin, which we had to take from him, for fear of its being spoilt. What a rage the little brute was in! He tore and dragged at his chain, turned head over heels, and bit and snapped at anything that came near him, and did not get quiet till late in the evening, when, apparently done up, he lay down and slept.

The morning of the 21st found us surrounded by ice once more, and we sighted several seals, but they seemed very wary, and kept a long way off; in fact, so far from us that all our shots were mere chance shots. At last, however, we sighted a fine big fellow lying on the ice, basking in the morning sun; so manning a boat, several of us went after him, and approaching cautiously, we got near enough to shoot him. We then landed to secure him; but Joe had his doubts about his being dead, and looked at it with a most comical expression, which made us all laugh. We, however, felt sure that he was quite dead, as the bullet had entered just to the left of the muzzle, and had passed through his head; so making a

rope fast to him, we dragged him down to
the boat, and, throwing him into the sea off
the floe, took him in tow.

We had not gone very far, however,
before he began to show signs of life, and
after turning over and over several times,
like a spinning-bait, he managed to get
free, and we thought we had lost our prize,
as he went down immediately. We at
once stopped the boat, and pulled over the
place where he had disappeared, when we
lay on our oars for several minutes, and he
soon reappeared not far from us perfectly
helpless, and once more apparently dead.
We now got him into the boat, but as he
was bleeding profusely from the head, one
of our men held it over the side, in which
position he looked as if he was nursing
some one who was very sea-sick.

On getting on board, we found that we

had neared a large floe with some fresh
water on it; so laying out a couple of ice-
anchors, we got the fire-engine on to the
ice, and began to pump fresh water on
board, but found that watering by buckets
was quicker work.

After finishing watering, we steamed for
several hours through large quantities of
ice, at last getting into a little clearer
water; but about ten o'clock that night,
we were enveloped in a very dense fog,
and, before we knew where we were, found
ourselves apparently getting into a thick
ice-pack. As we could not see anything
much farther than our jibboom end, our
only alternative was to retrace our course as
well as we could; but before we had gone
very far back in that direction, we came
across a great deal more ice, so that it was
evident that we were quite surrounded by

it. We now stopped the engines, and anxiously waited for the fog to lift, to show us how to get out of our awkward position. It cleared away a little before midnight, and we found ourselves entirely shut in by thick fields of ice, and not very far distant in the direction we wished to go appeared a very solid floe with, as far as we could see, but one lead through it, and that a very crooked one. We managed to force our way to its entrance, and though we had to wind our way through it for a considerable distance, it brought us into clearer water, and on Sunday forenoon we were able to steer once more on a straight course; but about noon we came again on a solid pack, through which we could find no lead. We made fast to it for two or three hours, when another floe began to drift on us; so hurriedly getting our ice-anchors on board, we steamed away before getting nipped by it. We were only just in time, as, having forced our way through several heavy lumps, and getting into a clear space of water, we looked back to where we had been lying, and saw nothing there but a large addition to the first floe.

We were now lying in a little bay formed by ice, in the middle of Lancaster Sound, with a "bolt hole" to the eastward, upon which we kept a watchful eye, for fear it should close and imprison us; whilst away to the westward appeared nothing but a solid mass of ice, and we began to fear that it would prevent all further progress. That evening Joe shot a young seal, which was very acceptable, as our stock of "seal-beef" was getting rather short, and though we had seen many

H

that day, this was the only one we succeeded in securing.

The next morning, getting out of our
little bay, we steamed along the edge of
the pack to the southward, hoping to find
some lead or other which should take us
once more towards the west. We at last
came to some loose ice, with clear water
showing on the other side; but though
the ice was all broken up, it was very
closely packed, and apparently there was
about half a mile of it which we would have
to force our way through. But our little
ship did it well! Slowly but steadily,
sometimes forcing her way like a wedge
between large pieces; at others, striking a
flat piece and running up on it, her weight
would cause it to break into small fragments; again, catching a large piece in
the centre (too solid to be broken), she

would force it forward some little distance until it had brought her to a standstill; in the latter case, she would have to be backed astern, and either dodge round the edge of it, or else, getting a little more way on her, we would make another attempt at splitting it. By noon we were in clear water, and once more our hopes were raised with the feeling that we might yet accomplish our aim. The glass began to fall, with every indication of a coming snow-storm.

Whilst at tea that evening, we came into collision with a small iceberg, through the negligence of the man whose duty it was to keep a good look-out. Fortunately for us, Toms happened to come up the hatchway, and looking out over the bows, saw it right ahead, and close to. He immediately sang out, " Hard a-starboard ! " to the man

at the wheel (Timpson), who obeyed the
order most smartly, so that instead of
striking it end on, we struck it with
our starboard bow, glancing off it, but
with sufficient shock to startle and alarm
all hands, and make us all bolt on deck.
Our anchor was carried away from the cat-
head, but remained hanging by the shank
painter. This, thank God, was the only
damage done : had we struck full end on,
I doubt if the little *Pandora* would now
be lying in Southampton docks.

That night we were all turned up to
shorten sail, the fall of the barometer having
prophesied but too truly, and the snow
began to come down in heavy flakes; but
we were in hope that this wind would
leave us a clear passage on the south of
Lancaster Sound. About midnight our bear
managed to get loose, and as I was not on

deck to witness the exciting scene, I will insert Captain Young's description of his recapture.

"August 24.

" We passed a most dismal night, the wind "increasing and howling in the rigging. " Snow and sleet also prevailed as we "scudded onward. We caught a glimpse of " the land apparently somewhere between " Sergeant Point and Cape York. It was " only for a moment, and then all was dark- " ness, and wind, and snow, and ice. In the " midst of this situation, our bear gradually " worked himself into a state of frantic ex- " citement, watching the floe ice rapidly " dashing past our sides, and in his attempts " to get over the bulwarks he released his " chain until it was evident that in a few " moments he would be free, whether to dive " overboard or to run a-muck among the

" watch appeared a question of doubt. The
" alarm being given by Pirie, who was
" writing up the deck log, the watch was
" called to secure the bear, and I fear that
" during the half-hour which elapsed the
" ship was left, more or less, to take care of
" herself. The whole watch, besides Pirie
" and myself, with a crowbar, attacked the
" unfortunate Bruin, whose frantic struggles
" and endeavours to attack everyone within
" reach were quite as much as we could
" control. He was loose, but, by a fortunate
" event, a running noose was passed round
" his neck, and the poor brute was hauled
" down to a ring-bolt until we could secure
" the chain round his neck and body. I
" had, hitherto, no conception of the strength
" of these animals, and especially of the
" power of their jaws; fearing that the iron
" crowbar might injure his teeth, I jammed

" a mop handle into his mouth while the
" others were securing his chain, and he bit
" it completely through. At last Bruin gave
" in, and beyond an occasional struggle to
" get loose and a constant low growling, he
" gave us no further trouble. I ought to
" mention that in the midst of the scrim-
" mage the doctor was called up to give
" him a dose of opium, in the hope of sub-
" duing him by this means, but having
" succeeded in getting him to swallow a
" piece of blubber saturated in chloroform
" and opium sufficient to kill a dozen men,
" our Bruin did not appear to have expe-
" rienced the slightest effect, and the doctor
" who volunteered to remain up, and ex-
" pressed some anxiety as to the bear's fate,
" retired below somewhat disappointed."

Our course amongst the ice had been
very much altered at different times, and

our compasses were now getting almost
useless, as every day brought us nearer to
the magnetic pole. The consequence of all
this was that, on sighting some cliffs that
forenoon through a break in the fog, we
thought they were those of Leopold Island
(which lies on the south side of Lancaster
Sound), but on the fog lifting a little more
for a short time, we found that we were on
the north instead of the south side of the
sound; so we kept her away, keeping the
land on our starboard hand, as by so doing,
if this were really the coast north of Lancaster Sound, we would be steering to the
west.

That afternoon Pirie got an observation
for longitude, which showed us that we
were a little to the eastward of Maxwell
Bay, but all that day it was very thick, the
fog only occasionally lifting and showing

us land on the starboard beam. The next
forenoon the fog was so thick that we had
to lie to for some time, but about noon we
were able to keep away, it having cleared
up slightly. About tea-time the fog cleared
away altogether, and we passed close to
Cape Ricketts, a magnificent cliff rising
perpendicularly from the sea to the height
of several hundred feet. De Wilde obtained a pretty good photograph of it, but
though the sea was rather quiet, there was
too much motion to enable him to produce
as satisfactory a copy as he would have
desired.

Soon after this we sighted Cape Riley,
and farther on the high cliffs of that historic
place—Beechey Island. On rounding Cape
Riley, we appeared to have come in sight of
a deserted settlement, for though there was
only one house to be seen (which had been

built twenty-three years ago), on the beach
lay two boats and a small cutter yacht, and
in front of the house a flagstaff, worn white
with age, showed itself conspicuously against
the dark cliffs behind.

We steamed into Erebus Bay, and anchored abreast of Northumberland House,
that being the name given to the small
wooden structure built by Captain Pullen,
commander of the *North Star*, in 1852 :
but there was no boat to come out to
welcome us, no pilot to offer his services,
no natives crowding alongside in their
kyaks, wanting to sell us curiosities or fresh
food ; the rattle of our cable, as it ran
through the hawse-pipe, and our own voices
being the only sounds which broke this
awful stillness. We seemed to have come
into the land of the dead, and truly,
I think, it may be called so, for here no

living person dwells, whilst on this spot lie five graves side by side, and a small octagonal wooden pillar erected near the house has, on each side, the names of those who have perished in Arctic exploration engraved on zinc and nailed to it, a rough, yet a touching monument. At the foot of this is placed a marble tablet to the memory of Sir John Franklin and all who perished with him, sent out by Lady Franklin, and placed here by Sir Leopold M'Clintock.

It was now eleven o'clock at night, and we made preparations for landing ;* so while the boat was being got ready, the landing party satisfied the inner man with beef-tea, coffee, and biscuit. On landing, we walked up to the house, Captain Young

---

* The reader must remember it was broad daylight.

saying to me as he went up the beach,
"Look out, it is as likely as not that we
shall find a bear inside," there being evi-
dence of these Arctic thieves having bur-
glariously entered it and dragged out some
of its valuable contents. However, we had
no chance of dealing summary justice to
these spoilers, as they had all absconded;
but what a state they had left the house in!
Almost the whole of one side had been
broken down; bales of flannel and serge
had been dragged for several yards, and
having been torn open, the contents had
been spread out over the boats (which lay
close to the house) and thrown about the
beach, as a washerwoman would lay out
her clothes to dry, whilst one bale, which
the bears did not appear to understand how
to unpack, had been bodily rolled for
several yards farther. Casks had been

tumbled over, the heads knocked in, and the contents no doubt demolished. They also appeared to have had fine games with the pemmican tins, which were lying in all directions, and, though made of very stout tin, were perforated in several places with their claws and teeth, but evidently Bruin was unable to get a meal out of them.

The first thing we did on entering the house was to look for records or any papers that might have been left to show who had been the last visitors to this island, and more especially we searched for a paper which had been nailed to the back of the door by Sir Leopold M'Clintock when in command of the *Fox*, giving a list of the contents of the house, and also noting that which he had taken away. The bears, however, appeared to have understood the proper entrance, and finding the door locked, and not possessing a skeleton key, nor having been initiated into the mystery of lock-picking, they broke it down and smashed it into so many pieces that it was impossible to distinguish it from the rest of the débris. The minutest search failed to find this paper. The snow having been driven in for eighteen winters had formed a large frozen mound covering almost everything contained in the house, and holding all casks, bales, and cases as firmly as if they had been imbedded in rock. But we did not try to get out anything that night, our object being simply to see in what state of preservation everything was. We came across a boat's magazine hanging to one of the beams of the house, and on opening it found several papers which had been left by the different Franklin search expeditions, one of which told us that all

the cairns built on that island had evidently
only been built for surveying purposes, and
contained no records; also stating that
there were several other papers in the post
office, which said post office was a small
hole cut in the before-mentioned post, which
served as a monument to those who had died
in these regions. Old Florence was told off
to boil water so as to be able to cook some
pemmican, as we knew we were sure to be
hungry in a short time, whilst several of us
went off to examine the *Mary* yacht, which
lay some distance off hauled up on the beach.
We found her in very good order, though her
decks and spars were much weatherworn.
We next examined the boats, which we
found could be made seaworthy after a few
repairs, and felt satisfied that, should we
have to abandon or should we lose our
ship, we had a good retreat to fall back

upon.   We then returned to the house and
sat down under the lee, to examine the
papers which were in the magazine, and
cold work it was, even though we were
sheltered from the wind.

We now regaled ourselves with pemmican, after which we returned on board,
and it being then about 3 A.M., and all
being very tired, turned in, and slept
soundly until seven o'clock, when, after
a good breakfast, we prepared to land
once more.   I was left on board to take
charge of the ship, as Pirie had to go
and take observations, and we landed what
boats and men we could spare to take on
board such stores as Captain Young might
think requisite for us, in addition to our
own, in case we should have to winter out
here.   All that day we were hard at work
getting provisions on board.   In the after-

noon I was enabled to go on shore, and after work was over, several of us went to visit the graves, which lay about a mile and a half from the house. There were five of them altogether, two of which were those of the men who belonged to the Franklin expedition. On one head-stone the inscription was utterly effaced, leaving no record of the poor fellow whose remains had been there interred.

After all our provisions were on board, and we had had tea, we got under way, and with a fair wind under steam and sail we proceeded towards Peel Sound, but the next morning, just as we were close to some thick ice, a dense fog came on, which effectually hid it from our sight; so we had to ease our engines. This was about 4 A.M., and Toms having relieved me, I was very glad to get below and turn in, being very

I

tired from having been up nearly the whole of the previous night. On awaking the next morning, I found we were in the middle of this ice, and though still thick, we were making our way through it, but that forenoon we had a great deal to contend with.

About noon we made fast to a large floe piece, from which we got a little water, and after dinner pushed on once more, and got on very well, until at 10 P.M., when we came upon a solid pack, stretching as far as the eye could see, without the sign of a lead through it, and no water to be seen beyond. We made fast to a detached floe piece close to with the intention of waiting until things looked brighter. Next morning we shifted from this floe piece to the solid pack, and began to lay in another stock of fresh water from several pools on it. We turned

Made fast to a pack near Limestone Island.

Page 114.

all our dogs out to have a good run, and De Wilde took a photograph of the ship as she was lying there, and also one of Limestone Island, which could be seen in the distance. After staying two or three hours, a lead suddenly appeared to open out some two miles distant, as if it had been purposely made for us; so calling all hands on board, Captain Young got ready to start, but our dogs did not seem at all inclined to return to their prison, and though we succeeded in catching most of them, one, in a very insubordinate manner, seemed determined not to obey orders. He would come close alongside when called, but all the coaxing in the world would not get him over the plank which was placed as a bridge for his special benefit.

We then landed two or three men to go in rear of him and prevent his escape, and, placing tempting pieces of seal meat along the plank, hoped to entice him on board; but he was too cunning! He would crawl up gradually to the edge of the plank, and the moment he had secured the nearest piece of meat in his mouth, he would bolt, cleverly eluding all endeavours on the part of our men to catch him.

Captain Young therefore called all hands on board, and ordered them to hide themselves, with a hope that on feeling himself deserted he would come on board, but to no purpose; so we resorted to the expedient of landing another dog with a long tether as a sort of decoy. This proved successful; so getting our deserter on board, we started for the above mentioned lead.

We were not long steaming through it, and found rather clearer water on the other side of this large pack, and that afternoon

we got close up to Limestone Island. After
having worked through a little more ice
which lay around the island, Captain
Young, the doctor, Beynen, and I, here
landed, with the hope of finding a depot
of provisions which had been left there
some years before by one of the previous
expeditions. Beynen and the doctor
walked along the beach on the south
side, whilst Captain Young and I started
for the top. About halfway up the
sloping side of the island, we came upon
a large pile of stones, which had evidently
been placed there by human hands ; but
on pulling them down, we found no tin
or record of any description. We had,
unfortunately, forgotten to take pickaxe
or shovel ; so we both obtained flat stones,
and, kneeling down, began to grub into
the soft gravel (like two dogs scraping at a

rabbit-hole), with the hope of finding something buried beneath it, but to no purpose;
and our time being precious, we called two
of our boat's crew up from the beach,
and set them to work burrowing, whilst
we continued our ascent with the hope
of being able to ascertain, from the summit of the island, in what condition the
ice was in Peel Sound. But on our
arrival there such a thick fog had come
on that nothing could be seen. We sat
down for a few minutes to regain breath,
but a thick kind of Scotch mist was gradually wetting us through; so we did not
stay long, but returned to see whether
our men had been successful in finding
anything. They had managed to dig a
large deep hole, but found nothing, so
building up the cairn again, and making
it much larger, we placed a record of our

own in it. The doctor joined us here, and informed us that he had found the remains of an Esquimaux village on the beach; so after visiting it, we returned on board, and, steaming round, between the island and " North Somerset," we proceeded down Peel Sound. The ice we passed that night was very heavy, but we slipped through between it and the land; the next morning found us steaming down the sound (or rather I should say Peel *Straits*) in perfectly clear water.

It is still a disputed point whether Sir John Franklin's ships got down these straits, or whether he passed round to the north of Cape Walker and down M'Clintock Channel. If the latter, we can claim the honour of being the first who had ever navigated these waters, although the coast line for some distance had been surveyed with sledging parties under the command of Sir James Ross and Sir Leopold M'Clintock, and Captain Allen Young had connected their farthest with Bellot Straits during the winter he was out there in the *Fox*.

That evening we were on a fresh lookout for a cairn, which had been erected by Sir James Ross and Sir Leopold M'Clintock, at the most southern point which they had reached in the above mentioned surveying expedition, and sighting it at about half past eight, Captain Young, Pirie, Beynen, and McGahan landed, to search for the record, which they found in a most perfect state of preservation, after being deposited there for a period of twenty-six years, it having been left in June 1849. The paper was as white, and the writing as clear, as if it had been written yesterday, the ink not even having faded. Leaving a record in its place, they returned on board, and we stood on again for the southward, keeping along the coast of North Somerset, and in the middle watch sighted two islands on our starboard bow. It was just light enough to distinguish them, and also to discern the coast line which lay on our port hand; but as we neared these islands, a thick fog came down, shutting out everything from our sight. There we were, knowing that we had the land close to on the port side, these two islands close to us on the starboard bow, wrapped up in fog, with our compasses utterly useless. I never felt so utterly lost in my life. I can only liken the feeling to that of a person groping about in a dark room, and knowing that at any moment he might tumble up against

some of the furniture. To proceed on
would have been madness ; so stopping
the engines, I went down and called the
captain. He asked me if there was any
wind, and on telling him that what little
wind there was was right ahead, he
ordered me to put her before it and let her
drift back as nearly as possible in the
direction from which we had come, he
himself coming on deck, and remaining up
for the rest of the night. Had there been
no wind, or had this wind shifted, we
should not have known, in the least, in
which direction our ship's head pointed,
and we should have been rather perplexed
as to our whereabouts. As it was, we were
trusting our steering to the wind remaining
in the same direction, it being utterly impossible to tell whether it did shift or not.

Early in the morning, however, the fog

lifted, and we were able to resume our voyage. That forenoon we passed several islands, and there being clear water ahead as far as we could see, our hopes rose high with the thought that the afternoon would find us as far south as Bellot Straits. We could think and talk of nothing else but of our success, and at dinner that day it formed the chief topic of our conversation, but Captain Young rather threw cold water on our hopes by telling us not to feel so sure of it, as at any moment we might come on a pack which we might find impenetrable. His words were almost prophetic, for on returning on deck after dinner, we saw ahead of us, stretching from land to land, what McGahan in his correspondence to the *New York Herald* appropriately calls the " dreaded " ice blink, and before long we sighted the ice itself. There it lay, a perfect barrier across these straits, and our spirits, which had been so high a short time before, now fell equally as low. However, it was no use grumbling; so we had to "grin and bear it." Making fast to this pack, we waited with a vain hope that our former luck would not desert us, and that in a short time a lead might show itself.

This was certainly the thickest pack we had encountered, the edge of it, to the depth of about a quarter of a mile, being formed of innumerable broken up lumps of very thick ice, with occasionally here and there a large floe like that to which we were made fast, all jumbled together, whilst behind all this, about a quarter of a mile distant from where we lay, was to be seen a solid wall of ice, extending as far as the eye could discern from our mast-head.

All this loose ice to which I have ad-verted was in perpetual motion, and kept up a rumbling noise whilst the pieces were grating and grinding against each other; but the worst of it was that it was ice which we could neither steam through, take a boat through, nor drag a sledge or boat over, for even fifty yards.

Beynen, McGahan, and I took the dingy, and went away along the edge of it with the hope of being able to get a seal, several of these wily customers occasionally show-ing their heads above water for a few minutes. We pulled away for some dis-tance, and it was curious to listen to those talking on board, their voices being heard for a greater distance in that climate than is usual in most parts of the world. We had two or three shots at the seals, but it is very difficult to strike so small an object as a seal's head from any boat, more especially from such a cranked little thing as our dingy, and the result being that we did not obtain any. We pulled into a small bay in the ice, and landed on a floe piece just to stretch our legs, but had scarcely left the boat when we saw those big blocks of ice I have before mentioned regularly waltzing down towards her, so without hesitation we jumped into her and got out of the way as quickly as we could, though we had a little difficulty in getting quite clear of them. It gave us a good insight into the rapidity with which ice travelled, there being apparently no motive power, and but a very slight breeze at that time, in fact, almost a calm, and there appeared to be no current to affect our boat. Therefore, the only thing we could judge was that there was an under current which acted on the immersed parts of these floating fragments. A breeze, however, soon sprang up, and perhaps this might have had something to 'do with it. We returned on board, but that evening these loose pieces had commenced forming a barrier on the other side of us; so we had to cast off and make our way into clear water again for fear of being beset, and we then laid to for the night with the hope that on the morrow we might find ourselves in a better position. The next day, however, instead of showing us any alteration in the ice, came upon us with a thick fog, which, however, cleared a little in the afternoon, and we found ourselves among a shoal of white whales, which came playing round the ship. They were very restless, and did not remain quiet for any time.

I went away in a whaler to see if we could harpoon one of these fellows, but with very small hope, and though we managed to get pretty near one of them, he was too far off for a shot. The fog having completely cleared away, and the ice broken up a great deal towards Roquette Islands, we saw the ship steaming towards them, and as we were between her and them, she picked us up on her way. We got near enough to the islands that evening for a boat to be able to land; so Captain Young went ashore and climbed to the top of the highest, where he built a cairn and left a record. Pirie also landed with him, and was able to take a rough survey of these islands.

From the top of this island they were able to get a better view of the ice than we could from the mast-head, and though they must have been able to see for a distance of many miles, there was not a sign of water anywhere to the southward. There was nothing but one unbroken mass of solid ice.

The failure of our enterprise now appeared to stare us in the face, and we felt it doubly so that evening when the ice began forcing its way to the northward, evidently under the influence of a southerly gale, which must have been blowing on the other side of this enormous pack. The next afternoon, however, though the ice on each side of the straits was well to the northward of us, there was enough clear water in the wake of the islands for us to get near enough to them in the ship to send a boat on shore. Captain Young and I landed, to have another look at the ice, with the faint hope that we might see a break in it somewhere. But on reaching

K

the summit of the island on which we
had landed, there was not a sign of water
to be seen to the southward, whilst to the
northward the ice stretched out along each
coast of these straits, looking like the arms
of some gigantic monster stealthily en-
deavouring to embrace our little ship and
hold her there until it was his pleasure to
let her go.

But we could not wait long on shore,
as we perceived the floating ice fast drifting round the *Pandora*, and we knew that
at any moment our communication with
the ship might be cut off—perhaps for
ever. So we made for our boat again, as
fast as our legs would allow us over the
rough and broken ground. Pirie managed
to keep the ship very close to us, though
it must have been hard work amongst this
thick loose ice which had regularly surrounded him, and when we had got on

board, it was with no little difficulty that
we managed to get her once more into
clear water.

I will here quote a portion of Captain
Young's journal for that day :—

"Peel Straits, September 1.

"We are in a deep bight in the ice.
"All southward one unbroken pack from
"side to side. Fitzroy Inlet full. Bellot
"Straits packed close. The spring tides
"have passed away, and there is no hope of
"getting farther south this season, for the
"winter has already set in with the usual
"accompaniment of gales, sleet, and snow,
"and the new ice is rapidly forming on
"the waters. I am very loth to turn back,
"and am struggling on against hope, if
"ever to reach Bellot Straits, where we
"could hold on in comparative security

K 2

"longer than we could possibly do here.
" To remain in our present position in Peel
" Straits is out of the question, as well as
" purposeless.   We are hourly in danger of
" being beset, and, once beset, are impri-
" soned for the winter, without a harbour,
"and in a position which would leave us
" powerless to accomplish anything.   From
" this position we could merely follow by
" sledging in the spring the footsteps of
" that veteran explorer, M'Clintock, to King
" William Land, under the same conditions,
" without hope of further result, and in that
" case we should run the risk of the ship
" not being released next summer, and
" a consequent autumn return, probably
" ending our hitherto successful voyage in
" disaster."

That night, in the middle watch, the

ice drifted so rapidly to the northward
that we had to put the ship before the
wind, and keep on ahead of it, the consequence being that we were soon driven
twenty miles to the northward of Bellot
Straits. In the forenoon a north-west
wind sprung up strong, and brought large
masses of floe ice down with it at a rapid
rate; but from whither? We passed none
on our way south that could have come
down here in that short time, and the
only way we could account for this ice is
that it must have come out of Browne's
Bay and other bays along the westward
sides of these straits. It was " the last
straw to break the camel's back," as we knew
that this ice was rapidly drifting down on
the top of the barrier which we had just
left, thus making all chances of our getting
to the southward utterly hopeless.

We now encountered a northerly wind, which we had to beat against for some way under fore and aft sail and steam, through large quantities of rapidly drifting ice. That afternoon a shift of wind enabled us to set close-reefed topsails.

Our great anxiety was whether we should get out of Peel Straits, or be shut up, like a rat in a trap, for the winter by the ice which was always drifting to the eastward in Bellot Straits. Captain Young, in his journal, describes our escape in the following words :—

" We are running back under reefed " sails out of Peel Straits. The tempera- " ture is 26 degrees, with squalls and snow. " We stop to sound occasionally the un- " explored depths of this sea, on which no " ship has ever been known to sail, and " by the evening of the 4th, we were pass-

"ing around Limestone Island, the tempe-
"rature falling to 24 degrees. As we ap-
"proach an enormous pack which lies close
"to us on our port hand, and threatens
"completely to cut off our retreat, I could
"just see at intervals between the snow
"storms a small thread of water, perhaps
"half a mile wide, and I determined to run
"a race against time with the pack, and
"try to pass Cape Rennel before it im-
"pinged completely on the land by the
"action of the north-west gale that was
"blowing. It was, in fact, our only chance
"of getting out of the straits, for had we
"hesitated or stood back to the south-west,
"we should certainly have been shut in for
"the winter; so we pressed on with the
"fast increasing darkness and gloom of the
"coming winter night.

"It was a dreadful night, the wind in-

" creased to a violent gale, with hail, and
" sleet, and blinding drifts, and we threaded
" our way in the dark, the white glare of
" the pack on one hand, the gleam of the
" snow-clad land on the other being our
" guide.   Once only during the night a
" solitary star shone out for half an hour,
" giving the helmsman a point for the
" direction of the ship.   As the wind in-
" creased, the temperature fell to 18 degrees
" F., and the spray froze over the ship as
" it fell, and by midnight our decks were
" full of snow, which whirled up in blind-
" ing drifts from the eddy winds out of
" the sails.   We could from time to time
" judge our progress along the coast by
" the excellent description of Ross and
" M'Clintock in their spring journey.

    " Thus at 10 P.M. we passed the deep
' gorge which separates the limestone from

" the red sandstone formation, a curious
" geological feature of the coast.   By mid-
" night we were off Cunningham Inlet, and
" by 3 A.M. we were just in the position I
" had so long dreaded.   The ice pack had
" already impinged on Cape Rennel, leaving
" not the slightest passage, and our progress
" in this direction was stopped.   Suddenly
" a snow storm, which had been beating
" down upon us for the whole night, abated,
" and disclosed the high, precipitous cliffs,
" hanging immediately over us, presenting
" a most ghostly appearance, the horizontal
" strata seeming like the huge bars of some
" gigantic iron cage, and standing out from
" the snow face.   In fact, it was the skele-
" ton of a cliff, and we appeared to be in
" its very grasp.   For a few minutes only
" we saw this apparition, and then all was
" again darkness.   We barely had room to

" round to between this cliff on one side
" and the pack on the other, and then
" hastily ranged about seeking some escape.

 " Most providentially, after three hours
" of intense anxiety, a slight movement in
" the pack was reported from aloft, giving
" indications of a weak place in the pack.
" The ship was instantly turned in that
" direction, and eventually we succeeded in-
" forcing her through the weakest place in
" this nip, now our only hope, which was
" already rapidly closing again with the
" formation of new ice."

After passing Cape Rennel, we ran
before a fair gale out of Lancaster Sound,
but on getting to the entrance of the
Sound, we found it blowing from the northward. Captain Young having determined
on paying a second visit to the Carey
Islands, with the hope of this time find-

Rounding Cape Warrender in a Gale.

ing news of the *Alert* and *Discovery*, there
was nothing for it but to haul to the
wind under close-reefed topsails, and do
our best to beat up in the teeth of this
bitter northerly gale.

The following is the description of it
from Captain Young's own pen :—

" We have just passed through a gale
" with the temperature down to 28 degrees,
" and we were iced all over, for the heavy
" seas beat upon us and froze as they fell
" on our sides and decks, and the *Pandora*
" became one huge icicle. Anchors, shrouds,
" and rigging were one solid mass. It be-
" came a serious question how long we
" could have manœuvred the ship, had the
" gale not abated. We had run out of
" Lancaster Sound beating up to the Carey
" Isles, where I determined to make a
" further effort to find some record of the
" *Alert* and the *Discovery*, by searching

" even every island of the group in detail,
" and failing in that, at all hazards, to make
" a dash for Littleton Island, feeling how
" anxious the friends of the expedition would
" be to hear news of their passage through
" the dangers of Melville Bay.   In this I
" was fully supported by all my officers,
" who appreciated the importance of obtain-
" ing some tidings of the expedition.

    " We reached the Carey Islands on the
" 10th of September, beating up all the
" way against a strong northerly wind, and
" finally reaching the group in the midst of
" a violent snowstorm.   The sea here, and
" as far as could be observed to the north,
" where the action of the wind was felt,
" was quite clear of ice, and although ice
" was still rapidly forming in still water,
" I think I could have been able to reach
" as far north as Littleton Island.   This
" time we hove to off the south-east island,

Page 140.

Our Second Visit to the Carey Islands.

" on the top of which we perceived a cairn.
" The island, instead of presenting a view
" of bare stones, was now covered with a
" white mantle of snow, which had com-
" pletely changed its appearance. It was
" some 700 feet or 800 feet high, and
" very steep, but the snow served as a
" means of ascent in a place where other-
" wise it would have been impossible to get
" up. Lieutenant Lillingston and Beynen
" went ashore, and for half an hour we
" watched them climbing up the steep face
" of the mountain. At last they reached
" the cairn, where they remained only a few
" minutes, for we soon saw them rapidly
" descending to the water's edge. In a few
" minutes they returned with a tin tube
" containing a packet addressed to the
" Admiralty, evidently left by Captain
" Nares."

CHAPTER IV.

HOMEWARD BOUND.

"Oh! dream of joy! is this indeed
The lighthouse top I see?
Is this the hill? is this the kirk?
Is this mine own countree?"—*Coleridge.*

HAVING attained our object, we turned the
head of the little ship once more to the
southward, and, bidding farewell to the
Carey Islands (which we left in a heavy
snowstorm), started for home, with the
intention of touching at Discoe on our way
for a few days' rest, to fill up with water,
and make everything snug on board before
recrossing the Atlantic.

We reached Discoe on the 20th September,

and not having had much sport during our cruise, Pirie and I, with Toms and Andrews, started in the steam launch for Discoe fiords, with the hope of getting some wild-fowl shooting. We arrived there about midnight, when it was perfectly dark, and, groping our way into a sheltered bay, made fast to the rocks, and, wrapping ourselves up, lay down to sleep until daylight, when, after a short run on shore, to have a glance at the place we had entered on the previous night, we started up the fiord with the hope of a good day's shooting before us. We, however, only got a few birds, and as it rained incessantly, it rather damped the ardour of our spirits. On the whole it was a very jolly little picnic ; but we little knew what a night we had before us! Our shooting being over, we turned to rejoin the *Pandora,* but on getting to the

mouth of the fiord, we found it blowing a
gale of wind from the southward and eastward, which was dead in our teeth. There
were only two alternatives: either to return
to an Esquimaux village in the fiord, and
there put up until it had abated (which
might not have been for days), or to steam
against it with the hope that it would not
freshen any more. We chose the latter,
and after steaming for two or three hours,
we found we were getting along very well,
and had got halfway to Lievely. But darkness set in, the wind freshened, and the sea
rose higher, breaking much oftener than
when we had first started. The danger of
one of these breakers coming on board was
great, as from our boat not being a lifeboat,
had she filled, she would have gone down
under us owing to the weight of the
engines and boilers and coal in her. In

the darkness we were often unable to tell which were breakers and which were pieces of floating ice, and altogether it was an anxious time. We at last gained the promontory in which lies the harbour of Godhavn, but it was so intensely dark that we could not discern the entrance ; all that could be seen was one long line of heavy breakers, breaking on that iron-bound coast.

For a long time we steamed up and down outside these breakers, anxiously trying to find the entrance to the harbour, and at last we saw two icebergs showing out most beautifully white in the black night, which we recognised as two that had been aground for a long time in the harbour. Using these as a landmark, we steered direct for them, which brought our boat exactly into the entrance of it, between two lines of the heavy breakers, and we soon found our-

L

selves alongside our little ship. Most thankful we were to find ourselves there; Pirie and myself owning to each other that we had had grave doubts of ever seeing her again. Captain Young had been very anxious about us, more especially as a native had told him that he had seen us go in another direction to that in which we had gone, and he therefore would not have known which way to have gone had we been detained.

I may here mention that these icebergs, which had been aground in the harbour for months, and which had served us so admirably as a landmark, broke up into small fragments the next morning.

We left Discoe on the 24th of September, and had a very good passage down Davis Straits, a fair wind following us the whole time.

An amusing incident occurred one evening whilst running before a moderate breeze. The nights had got very dark, and we being all dressed in blanket suits looked in the darkness very much like a lot of Polar bears walking about on our hind legs. One of our men, having observed this, determined to play a trick on the man at the wheel ; so getting a piece of the chain that had belonged to the same piece as the bear was chained with, he crawled on all fours towards the wheel, rattling this chain as he went, an accomplice at the same time poking up our bear with a mop handle to make him roar. The trick succeeded beautifully. No sooner did the man at the wheel see this object approaching him than he naturally enough jumped to the conclusion that our Bruin had got loose. He did not stop to make sure, but, leaving the vessel to take care of herself, ran forward on the opposite side of the deck, crying out, " The bear's adrift ! the bear's adrift!"

The ship, being left alone without any one to steer her, would most probably have broached to, but the author of the joke, not only knowing this, but also being afraid that one of the officers might run up the ladder with a loaded pistol and shoot him in mistake for the bear, was soon on his hind legs and doing duty at the deserted wheel. Our friend who had run from his post had not the face to brave the chaff of his fellow shipmates forward, and turn the tables on the man who had so successfully frightened him, otherwise he might have left him to do his duty at the wheel for the rest of his appointed time.

Our fine weather was not to last for ever, and we had hardly got clear of Cape

Homeward Bound.   Heavy Weather.

Farewell before the wind began to increase in force, and we soon had to close-reef our topsails. Under these and our foresail we ran for some time, but each day the wind seemed to be gaining additional strength, and we had to take our foresail in. It was now blowing a perfect hurricane, and the seas breaking over us continually forced us to batten down. In this condition we remained for five days. Fortunate for us that we had battened down, as one morning, when the hands were at breakfast, an enormous sea pooped us. Towering up for a second over our stern, it burst in one large volume on board us, and rushing along the whole length of our decks, leapt up on the top-gallant forecastle and emptied the greater body of itself over the bows in a cloud of foam and spray. So much, however, remained on our deck as to leave us

for a few seconds as if water-logged, and I
thought it impossible that the ship could
rise over the next one that was coming up
astern fast. Providentially she did, and by
the time the third one had overtaken her,
she had freed herself of so much of the first
as again to appear to have some life in her,
and we were once more flying before this
hurricane and such seas that I have never
before witnessed in any part of the world.

We carried this gale to the entrance of
the Channel, where we got less, and more
variable, wind ; and we could not have had
a finer day than that which saw us drop
our anchor at Spithead, the 16th October
1875, after our short but interesting cruise.

Captain Young and myself landed, and
were most kindly received by Sir Leopold
and Lady M'Clintock.

I soon found myself in the train on my

way to London, having been sent up to the Admiralty with the despatches found at the Carey Islands, and was most cordially received by Mr. Ward Hunt.

And now, kind reader, farewell! with many thanks for having followed me so far in my attempt to give a description of our voyage north. Should it prove of any interest to even a few of its readers, the author will feel that his endeavours have not been utterly thrown away.

THE END.

PORTSMOUTH: J. GRIFFIN AND CO., 2 THE HARD.

The material originally positioned here is too large for reproduction in this reissue. A PDF can be downloaded from the web address given on page ivof this book, by clicking on 'Resources Available'.

For EU product safety concerns, contact us at Calle de José Abascal, 56–1°, 28003 Madrid, Spain or eugpsr@cambridge.org.

www.ingramcontent.com/pod-product-compliance
Ingram Content Group UK Ltd.
Pitfield, Milton Keynes, MK11 3LW, UK
UKHW012342130625
459647UK00009B/472